Broadman & Holman Publishers
Nashville, Tennessee
First Published in 1998 by ADC International, Belgium
This edition published under arrangement with
Ottenheimer Publishers, Inc., Owings Mills, Maryland
© 1998 A.M. Lefevre, M. Loiseaux, M. Nathan-Deiller, A. Van Gool
Editorial Director: CND/Muriel Nathan-Deiller
All rights reserved. Printed in Dubai.
BI085MLKJIHGFEDCB

THE GREATEST STORIES EVER TOLD

The Best Loved Stories From The Bible

BROADMAN
& HOLMAN
PUBLISHERS

THE CREATION OF THE WORLD

In the beginning, God created the heavens and the earth. All was dark, and deep water covered the land. God's Spirit was hovering over the water. Then God said, "Let there be light!"

At once bright rays of light shone down gently on the earth. God saw that this was good, and he separated the light from the darkness. He called the light "day" and the darkness "night." This was the first day.

Then God said, "Let there be a sky to separate the waters, so that water is above the sky and below the sky." And it was so. Night fell, and a new morning dawned. This was the second day.

(Genesis 1:1-8)

6

On the third day God said, "Let the waters below the sky gather together and let dry ground appear."

God called this dry ground "land" and the waters "sea." And at God's Word grass and plants grew across the earth. Flowers blossomed and trees bearing rich fruit burst toward the sky.

On the fourth day God placed the sun in the sky to bring warmth and light to the earth. Night fell and God created the stars and the moon to fill the darkness above the earth.

On the fifth day God said, "All kinds of fish shall fill the oceans, and birds shall fill the sky." And so the birds and the fish were the first creatures to live on the earth.

*(**Genesis 1**:9-23)*

On the sixth day God said, "Now the earth shall be filled with life." From the greatest animal to the smallest insect, God made each creature and sent them to live in all four corners of the earth. "Now I will create a being in my own image," He said.

Then God created man in His image. He created both male and female. "You have power over all living things in the sky, on the earth, and in the sea," God told them.

God stopped and looked at all He had created. He said it was very good.

On the seventh day God finished His work. He made this day holy, for this was the day He rested from His work.

*(**Genesis 1**:24-31; **2**:1-3)*

DAM AND EVE

God had planted on earth a beautiful garden, called Eden. He had created the garden for Adam, and here He placed the most wonderful plants and creatures.

God set Adam in the garden and said: "Everything in this garden is yours. Enjoy it and be happy. Only one thing is forbidden to you. The tree of the knowledge of good and evil grows in this garden. You must never eat any of the fruit from this tree. If you do, you will die."

Looking at the man He had created, God thought, "It is not right that Adam should be alone." So while Adam slept, God took one of his ribs. From this rib He made the first woman, Eve.

Adam and Eve were naked, but they were not ashamed, for this is how God had created them.

*(**Genesis 2**:4-25)*

Of all the animals that lived in the garden of Eden, the serpent was the most crafty.

"Wouldn't you like to know the secret of this fruit?" he whispered to Eve. "It will give you the knowledge of good and evil, which only God knows. That is why He does not want you to eat it, for then you could be as powerful as He!"

Adam and Eve knew that God had forbidden them to eat the fruit. But Eve thought about the wisdom that could be theirs, and she was tempted.

At last Eve picked one of the fruits, and tasted it. She passed it to Adam, who also ate some of the forbidden fruit.

*(**Genesis** 3:1-6)*

At once their eyes were opened. They saw that they were naked, and for the first time they felt ashamed. They sewed fig leaves together to hide their bodies. When God saw them, He was angry. "Who taught you that you were naked?" He demanded.

"Eve gave me the fruit!" said Adam, and Eve cried, "The serpent tricked me!"

God placed a curse on the serpent, then turned to Adam and Eve. From now on your life will be full of suffering," He said in a terrible voice. "You have disobeyed me, and from this moment the garden of Eden is forbidden you."

God drove Adam and Eve out of the garden. God placed an angel with a flaming sword at the entrance to the garden to stop them from ever returning.

*(**Genesis 3**:7-24)*

CAIN AND ABEL

After they left the garden of Eden, Adam and Eve had two sons, Cain and Abel. The eldest, Cain, farmed and grew crops for food, while Abel tended the sheep.

After a time, Cain became jealous of his brother. "God must love him more than me," he thought to himself. One day Cain's jealousy got the better of him, and he attacked and killed Abel.

When God asked him where Abel was, Cain answered, "I am not my brother's keeper!" But God knew very well what Cain had done and was angry at him. However, God did not want Cain to be killed, so he placed a special mark upon him to protect him.

*(**Genesis 4**:1-16)*

Noah's Ark

As the years passed, God watched sadly as mankind became idle and wicked. The only good people in all the world were Noah and his family. "I am going to destroy every living thing on earth," God told Noah. "For mankind must be punished for its wickedness."

God told Noah that he was going to send a huge flood to cover the earth, but that Noah and his family would be spared. "You must build an ark, and into this ark you must lead pairs of every creature. When the flood comes, these will be the only creatures to survive."

Bravely, Noah and his family set to work to build the ark as God had commanded.

*(**Genesis 6**:5-22; **7**:1-9)*

As soon as the last animals had boarded the ark, God closed the door. At once the rain began to pour, and the seas and rivers overflowed, lifting the ark above the ground.

The flood continued for forty days and forty nights until the earth was completely covered with water. Every living thing on the earth drowned and died, as God had intended. Only Noah and his family and the animals on the ark survived. At last the rain stopped.

After many months, the floodwaters began to go down slowly. The ark rested on a mountain. Noah sent out a raven to try to find dry land. Noah then sent out a dove. But the dove could not find dry land and returned to the ark.

*(**Genesis** 7:10-24; **8**:1-9)*

23

Noah sent out the dove again. This time the dove returned carrying a tiny olive branch in its beak. "We are saved!" cried Noah.

He waited seven days, then released the dove. It did not return, and Noah realized that the dove found a place to rest. The level of the water dropped still further, and at last Noah opened the door. Noah, his family, and all the animals went out of the ark.

Then God promised Noah, "Never again will I destroy the earth with a flood. And every time rainclouds appear over the earth, I will place a rainbow in the sky. This will serve as a sign to remind all creatures of my promise."

(*Genesis 8*:10-19; *9*:8-17)

ABRAHAM

Abraham was descended from Shem, Noah's eldest son. He lived with his wife Sarah in a village near Babel. One day God spoke to Abraham. "Abraham," He said, "You must leave your home and go on a long journey. Gather all the provisions you can carry, and take your wife and servants with you. I am going to lead you to the country that I have chosen for you."

Abraham obeyed at once and led his household across Mesopotamia and through Egypt. Every night they slept under the stars, and at last they reached the land of Canaan.

*(**Genesis 12**:1-5)*

In Canaan, God spoke again to Abraham. "You will live here, and your children and grandchildren after you."

"How is this possible, Lord?" asked Abraham in surprise. "Sarah and I are very old, and we have no children!"

"Abraham," said God sternly, "Do you doubt my word?" Soon afterward Abraham and Sarah had a son and they named him Isaac.

Some time later, God tested Abraham. God told Abraham that he must kill his son as a sacrifice. Abraham loved Isaac, and it was with great sadness that he obeyed God's command.

He was lifting his knife to kill the boy when God spoke again. "Let him go! If you are prepared to give me your only son, I see how much you must love me. You are truly blessed among men."

*(**Genesis 17**:1-8; **21**:1-3; **22**:1-19)*

JOSEPH AND HIS BROTHERS

Isaac's son, Jacob, had twelve sons of his own. Joseph was his father's favorite. When Joseph was seventeen, Jacob gave him a wonderful tunic. Joseph's brothers were very jealous, for this tunic was more beautiful than anything Jacob had ever given them. They wanted revenge.

One day, when they were working in the fields, the brothers seized Joseph and tore off his tunic. Joseph's oldest brother, Reuben, persuaded the others not to kill Joseph. At that moment some merchants came by on their way to Egypt. "This young man will make a good servant!" the brothers cried to the merchants. "Will you buy him from us?" The merchants agreed and took Joseph with them to Egypt.

The wicked brothers soaked Joseph's tunic in goat's blood and took it to their father. "Something terrible has happened!" they cried. "Joseph has been killed by a wild beast!"

(Genesis 37:2-33)

While he was a slave in Egypt, Joseph became known for telling people the meaning of their dreams. Even Pharaoh, the ruler of Egypt, came to see Joseph about a terrible nightmare he'd had. "Last night I dreamed of seven fat cows grazing on the banks of the Nile. Suddenly seven thin cows attacked and ate them."

Joseph said that God would give Pharaoh the answer. Joseph said, "The healthy cows mean that for the next seven years the harvests will be good, and there will be plenty of food. But for seven years after that, the harvests will be poor, and people will starve. This is a warning that you should save grain and corn to see you through the bad years."

Pharaoh was very grateful, and as a reward he put Joseph in charge of storing the crops. Joseph became a powerful minister.

*(**Genesis 41**:15-40)*

$\mathcal{M}$OSES

Jacob's descendants were called Israelites and Hebrews. Many of them lived in Egypt, and the new Pharaoh worried that they were becoming too powerful. "From now on, whenever a baby boy is born to the Hebrews, he must be killed," ordered Pharaoh cruelly.

Moses was born at this time, and his mother was afraid for his life. She wove a basket from rushes and carried it down to the river. Gently laying Moses inside, she placed the basket in the water among some rocks. His sister watched to see what would happen. Pharaoh's daughter found the basket among the reeds. She was as kind and gentle as her father was cruel. "This must be a Hebrew child," she said to herself. "His parents must want to save him very much." Pharaoh's daughter reared Moses as her own son.

*(**Exodus 1**:6-22; **2**:1-10)*

As Moses grew up, he saw that the Israelites were treated very badly. One day he saw a soldier beating one of his people. Moses was so angry that he hit the soldier very hard, and the man died. He knew that he had to leave Egypt and fled to Midian, where he became a shepherd.

One day he was out with his flock when a bush suddenly burst into flames. The flames burned brightly, but to his surprise the leaves and branches of the bush stayed green and fresh.

A voice spoke to him from the bush. "Moses, listen to me, for this is your God. Your people are suffering under Pharaoh, and you must lead them out of Egypt."

Moses was amazed. "But, Lord," he cried, "no one will listen to a poor shepherd like me!"

"Have faith," replied God. "Now go to Pharaoh."

*(**Exodus 2**:11-15; **3**:1-12)*

As God had commanded, Moses bravely asked Pharaoh to let the Israelites leave Egypt to worship God in the desert. But Pharaoh refused. "If you do not let us go, Egypt will suffer," Moses told him. But Pharaoh did not listen, and God sent a series of plagues to punish him.

First the Nile River and all the water in Egypt turned to blood. Then the land was infested with frogs. Then everything was infested with gnats, and flies filled the air. The animals died, except those owned by the Israelites, and all the Egyptians suffered painful sores and boils. A great hailstorm destroyed all the crops, and any plants left living were eaten by a huge swarm of locusts. God plunged the whole land into darkness, but still Pharaoh refused to let the Israelites go.

Finally God sent the most terrible plague of all. His angel visited every household and killed the firstborn male. But God had warned Moses, and the Israelite families were not harmed. At last Pharaoh agreed to let Moses lead the Israelites out of Egypt.

(Exodus 7-12)

Pharaoh soon regretted his decision to let the Israelites go. He sent a huge army to bring Moses and his people back to Egypt. When the Israelites saw the great army following them across the desert, they were afraid. "We should never have listened to you!" they complained to Moses. "We would rather be slaves in Egypt than die in the desert!"

"You must have faith," replied Moses. "The Lord will help us." When they reached the Red Sea, the Israelites thought they were truly lost, for there was no way to get across. Then, before their astonished eyes, the sea parted, leaving a clear path through the waves. "Thank the Lord!" cried Moses. "He has saved us!" Moses led the Israelites through the sea safely.

When Pharaoh's soldiers tried to follow, the great walls of water crashed down upon the army and swept it away.

*(**Exodus 14**:5-31)*

When the Israelites reached Mount Sinai, God spoke to Moses once more.

"Moses, these are my Commandments, which my people must obey. You shall have no other Gods but me. You shall not make and worship idols. You shall not speak my name with disrespect. The seventh day of the week shall be holy to you, and you shall not work on this day. You shall respect your parents. You shall not murder. You shall not commit adultery. You shall not steal or tell lies against your neighbor, nor must you envy what your neighbor possesses."

Moses came back down the mountain after forty days, carrying the Ten Commandments engraved on two tablets of stone. He found the Israelites worshiping a golden calf. Moses was very angry and ordered the statue destroyed.

(Exodus 19:20-21; 20:1-17; 32:1-20)

42

THE WALLS OF JERICHO

The tablets were kept in a beautiful wooden chest, specially built for the purpose. This was known as the Ark of the Covenant.

The Israelites continued their journey for many years. When they were nearly in Canaan, Moses called Joshua to him. "I am getting old," said Moses. "Soon I will go to God. Be strong and bold, Joshua, for you will lead our people to the promised land."

So Joshua led the Israelites into Canaan, and they came to the city of Jericho. The city gates were closed, and the people would not let the Israelites in.

"Carry the Ark of the Covenant around the city walls seven times," cried Joshua. As they walked, the priests sounded their trumpets. Then the people shouted, and the walls of Jericho came tumbling down, just as God had promised.

(Exodus 24-40; Deuteronomy 31:1-8; Joshua 5-6)

SAMSON & DELILAH

The Philistines were angry that the Israelites had returned to Canaan. They declared war on the Israelites, and many battles were fought. Samson, the leader of the Israelite army, loved Delilah, a Philistine woman. Samson was immensely strong, and one night Delilah asked him where his great strength came from. "It comes from God," he replied. "But if my hair were to be cut, I would become weak."

Delilah waited until Samson was asleep, then cut off his long hair. She sent for the guards, who arrested Samson. He was too weak to fight them, and they blinded him and took him to the Temple. "Oh Lord, show me your favor once more," prayed Samson. He stood between the two huge pillars of the Temple and began to push. God had not deserted Samson, and the Temple fell down upon the Philistines.

(Judges 16:4-30)

RUTH AND NAOMI

Since Samson's time, Canaan had become dry and arid, and there was a great famine in the land. Some of the Israelites returned south. One couple, Elimelech and Naomi, went to live in the neighboring country of Moab. They had two sons, and when these sons grew up they married local women. After many years Elimelech died, and shortly afterwards his two sons fell ill. They also died, leaving Naomi and her daughters-in-law with no one to help farm the land.

Naomi told her daughters-in-law that she was going to return to Bethlehem. "It is where I was born, and I belong there. You should go back to your parents. I am sure you will marry again." Orpah, the elder of the two women, said her sad goodbyes and left.

But Ruth, the youngest, would not let Naomi travel on her own. "Where you go, I go!" she told Naomi firmly.

*(**Ruth 1**:1-18)*

48

When they reached Bethlehem, Ruth promised Naomi that she would provide for them both. Each day she went out into the fields where the farmers were harvesting their crops and gathered up the wheat they had dropped.

Boaz, a rich relative of Naomi's, lived in Bethlehem. He had heard how Ruth looked after the old woman. One day he stopped Ruth in the fields. "Everyone here is talking of your kindness. You are a stranger here and your family is far away, yet you stay to take care of Naomi. You have a soul as beautiful as your face." He told her that she was welcome to collect wheat in his fields whenever she wanted, and Ruth was very grateful.

To Naomi's delight, Boaz and Ruth grew to love one another and were married.

(Ruth 1:19-22; 2-4)

Samuel

For many years the prophet Samuel guided the Israelites according to God's Word. However, as Samuel grew older, the Israelites decided that they needed a king to rule them. God was displeased that they were turning from him and told Samuel to give them a warning. "A king will make slaves of you and your children," said Samuel. "One day you will beg the Lord to save you from your king, but he will not heed you."

The Israelites refused to listen and chose Saul to be their king. At first Saul was a wise ruler, and God helped him win battles against the Philistines. But he grew proud and arrogant and began to forget God's Commandments.

God told Samuel to travel to Bethlehem. Here lived Jesse, the grandson of Ruth and Boaz. God had chosen David, Jesse's youngest son, to be the new king.

(1 Samuel 8-10; 15-16)

53

DAVID

Meanwhile, Saul's army was about to face the Philistines in another battle. The greatest soldier among the Philistines was called Goliath, who was taller and stronger than any other man. "Saul!" he cried out. "Let us decide the battle by single combat. Will any one of your men dare fight me alone?" Goliath was so huge that none of Saul's men had the courage to face him.

Suddenly David stepped forward. "I will fight the Philistine," he said.

Everyone was shocked, for David was just a young boy. He went forward to meet the giant wearing no armor and carrying only his sling. "Here I am, Goliath," he cried. "I am going to strike you down in God's name!"

Goliath was full of scorn for Saul's champion and reached for his spear. But David quickly took up his sling, and with a single stone he felled the mighty giant.

(1 Samuel 17:1-58)

David became so popular that Saul began to hate him. He told his son Jonathan, "Once I am dead, the people may try to make him king instead of you. Something must be done." But Jonathan loved David like a brother and warned him of his danger. "I know that you will be king in my place, for God has chosen you," he said. "But my father will try to kill you. You must hide."

When Saul learned of David's escape, he set after him at the head of a great army. One night, David crept into the king's camp and stole his spear and water jug. The next morning, when Saul realized how easily David could have killed him, he was ashamed.

He finally accepted that David would succeed him, and after Saul's death David was king for forty years. He ruled well and wisely from Jerusalem, which since then has been known as David's City.

(1 Samuel 18:1-30; 19:1-7; 24-26; 2 Samuel 5:1-10)

SOLOMON

David's son Solomon succeeded him as king. When Solomon was still a young man, two women came before him and asked him to settle their dispute. "Sire," said one. "Both our babies were born in the same house on the same day. Last night this woman's baby died. She stole my baby while I slept and says that my child died."

"I did nothing of the sort!" cried the other woman. "It was her baby who died!" Solomon thought for a moment. "There is only one solution to this problem," he said. "I shall cut the baby in two, and each of you shall have half."

One of the women nodded in agreement. The other cried out in horror. "No, don't kill the child!" she sobbed. "Let her keep the baby."

Solomon gave the child to the second woman. "Only a mother would rather give up her child than see it killed. The baby is yours." Soon Solomon's wisdom was famous throughout Israel.

*(**1 Kings 1**:28-30; **2**:9-12; **3**:16-28)*

Unlike other rulers, Solomon befriended the kings of neighboring countries, and there were no wars throughout his long reign. News of his wisdom spread far and wide.

The land was so peaceful and the people so content that Solomon decided they should build a great temple to God to show Him their thanks. The temple was built from limestone, and precious woods and metals were brought from afar. When the magnificent temple was completed, Solomon had the Ark of the Covenant carried inside. God told Solomon, "If you or your sons turn away from me and disobey my laws, I will destroy this temple."

Solomon ruled for forty years, and after his death the peace did not last. There were many wars, and God eventually allowed the great temple to be destroyed. This was a warning to the Israelites that they had forgotten God's Commandments once more.

(1 Kings 4:20-34; 5-8; 11:41-43; 2 Kings 24:20; 25:1-9)

ESTHER

After the destruction of Jerusalem, many Israelites fled to other countries. One man, Mordecai, traveled into Persia. Here he found work at the king's palace in Susa.

Unfortunately he soon fell afoul of Haman, the king's chief minister. Haman was very self-important and insisted that the workers bow down before him when he passed. Mordecai refused to do this, so Haman hated him. To get his revenge, Haman tried to turn the king against the Israelites. "There are too many of these people in your kingdom, Your Majesty," he told him. "I fear they may be dangerous."

With the king's authority, Haman planned to kill the Israelites. However, Haman did not know that Esther, the king's favorite wife, was herself an Israelite. Neither he nor the king knew that she was Mordecai's cousin.

(Esther 2:5-7, 17-18; 3:2-14)

Meanwhile, in the palace, Mordecai overheard two men whispering together. To his horror he realized that they were plotting to kill the king!

He hurried to tell Esther, who warned her husband of the plot. The two men were hanged. A short time later the king asked Haman, "What should I do for a man I want to honor?" Haman thought the king wanted to honor him. "Such a man should wear the king's robe and ride on the king's horse through the city square," replied Haman. "Then you must arrange for this event," commanded the king. "The man's name is Mordecai."

Later, at a royal feast, Esther explained to the king that the man who had saved his life was an Israelite. "His people are those Haman wants to destroy," she said, "and they are my people, too!" The king was furious with Haman and ordered him to be executed in Mordecai's place. Then he made Mordecai his minister.

(Esther 2:19-23; 6:1-14; 7:1-10)

DANIEL

Daniel was taken from his home in Judah to
Babylon when he was a teenager. Daniel had been
in Babylon sixty-five years. Because of his wisdom
and good character, he had been invited to serve
as an advisor to three different kings.

Darius the Mede was now king. He gave the
order that all his subjects must worship him as a
god or else be put to death. But Daniel continued
to worship the true God. Although Darius liked
Daniel and wanted him to be in charge of all of
Babylon, he had him thrown into a den of lions.
"Let your God save you," he said sadly.

The next morning he went to the lion's den,
expecting to find Daniel dead. To his surprise he
found Daniel without even a scratch on him.
Daniel told Darius that God had sent His angel to
keep the lions from hurting him. Darius was
happy. He told all his people, "Daniel's God is the
living God."
(*Daniel 1*:17-21; *2*:1-45; *3*:1-8; *4*:1-27; *5*:1-31; *6*: 7-28)

JONAH

In Canaan, God spoke to a man named Jonah. "The people in Nineveh are disobeying my Word," He said. He asked Jonah to go to Nineveh, in Assyria, and preach there. But Jonah was unwilling. "I don't like the people of Nineveh. I do not want God to forgive them," he complained to himself.

He tried to hide from God and traveled to the coast to catch a boat. Hardly had the boat left the shore when it was caught in a terrible storm. "God must be punishing me!" thought Jonah. At once he turned to the sailors and told them to cast him into the sea. "It is the only way you will be saved," he cried. As soon as Jonah plunged into the water, the wind dropped and the sea calmed. But at that moment an enormous fish rose up from the water and swallowed him!

For three days and three nights Jonah remained in the fish's stomach. Then the fish came to the shore and threw him on to the sand. Once again God told Jonah to go to Nineveh and preach there.

(Jonah 1:1-17; 2:1-10)

Jonah traveled to Nineveh and began to preach God's Word. He preached so well that all men learned from him, rich and poor alike. Soon the whole town was living according to God's Commandments, and God looked favorably on the people of Nineveh.

Once more Jonah began to complain to himself. "God loves these sinners too well," he thought. "They do not deserve his goodness."

Jonah was so angry he left town and went into the desert. While he slept, God made a tree grow beside him. Its shade protected him from the hot sun. Then God made the tree wither and die, leaving Jonah at the mercy of the sun's burning rays.

When Jonah asked why the tree had died, God explained to him. "Jonah, I know how happy you would be if this tree were to live again. Now imagine that the souls of the people of Nineveh were like this tree. When you first came to the town, their souls were shriveled and bare. Now they have heard my Word, and they grow strong and true. How much better is it that I have saved the souls of thousands of men, than that I should save one poor tree?"

(Jonah 3:10; 4:1-11)

70

MARY IS VISITED BY AN ANGEL

During King Herod's reign, a young woman lived in Galilee, in the town of Nazareth. Her name was Mary, and she was betrothed to a young carpenter called Joseph. One morning an angel appeared to Mary. "Do not be afraid, Mary," he said. "The Lord has sent me with a message for you. He has chosen to honor you above all women. Soon you will bear a son, whom you will name Jesus. He will be called the Son of the Most High, and his kingdom will last forever."

"How can this be," asked Mary in wonder, "since I am a virgin?" And the angel told her, "The power of the Holy Spirit shall come upon you, and you shall bear the Son of God."

Mary bowed her head. "I am the servant of the Lord," she replied. "It shall be as you have said."

(Luke 1:26–38)

THE BIRTH OF JESUS

The Israelites who had settled in Judea and Galilee were now known as the Jews, and Herod was their king. But the most powerful ruler in all the land was Augustus, the Roman emperor.

Some months after Joseph and Mary were married, Augustus wanted to know how many of his subjects lived in each country. He gave the order that all persons must return to the town of their birth, to sign a register. Joseph and Mary traveled to Bethlehem, where Joseph had been born.

But when they arrived, the inns were full, and they had to stay in a stable. Here, Jesus was born.

That night an angel appeared to a group of shepherds watching their flocks in the fields. "I bring you joyful news. Christ the Lord has been born to save mankind. You will find him in a stable, lying in a manger. Go now to Bethlehem and honor him."

*(**Luke 2**:1–20)*

THE VISIT OF THE WISE MEN

Far away in the East, wise men had seen a new
star in the heavens. They followed the star to
Jerusalem and came before King Herod. "We seek
the child who has been born King of the Jews,"
they told Herod. "We have come to worship him."
It had been foretold that the King of the Jews
would be born in Bethlehem. Herod asked the
wise men to send word when they had found the
child. "For I wish to honor him myself," he said.

When the wise men found Jesus, they bowed
before him and worshiped him. They had brought
him precious gifts of gold, frankincense, and
myrrh.

That night an angel came in a dream and
warned the wise men not to return to King Herod.
So they went back to their country without
traveling through Jerusalem.

(Matthew 2:1–12)

Herod had lied to the wise men, for he did not want to worship Jesus at all. He wanted to kill him. "The Jews will make him their king, and he will be more powerful than I!" he said.

When he realized that the wise men were not going to return, Herod was furious. He ordered his soldiers to go to Bethlehem and kill every boy child under two years of age. But the angel of the Lord appeared to Joseph in a dream and warned him: "Your child is in danger. You must take shelter in Egypt." Joseph took his family and left Bethlehem that same night, and they made the long journey into Egypt.

After some years in exile they learned that Herod was dead, and they returned to Nazareth.

*(**Matthew 2**:13–22)*

JESUS IN THE TEMPLE

Every year, Joseph and Mary went to Jerusalem to celebrate the feast of the Passover. When the festival finished, they would travel home with a large group of friends and family.

One year, when Jesus was twelve years old, his parents suddenly realized that he was not with them. Joseph and Mary hurried back to Jerusalem. Frightened for his safety, they searched for three days. Finally they found him in the temple, where he was talking with the priests and teachers. He amazed everyone with his knowledge and wisdom.

"We were so worried about you, my son," cried Mary. But Jesus replied simply, "You need not have searched for me. Where else would I be but in my Father's house?"

(Luke 2:41–52)

81

THE BAPTISM OF JESUS

Mary's relative, Elizabeth, also had a son. His name was John and he lived as a hermit on the banks of the Jordan River. People came from all over Judea to hear him preach and to beg forgiveness for their sins. After they had repented, he baptized them in the river; so he became known as John the Baptist.

John told his followers about the prophet Isaiah, who many years before had foretold that a savior would be sent to them. Some people thought that John was the savior. But he told them, "I baptize you with water, but one greater than I will baptize you with the Holy Spirit."

When Jesus was a young man, he went to John, who baptized him in the river. As Jesus stepped out of the water, the Holy Spirit came down upon him. The mighty voice of God spoke from heaven, "This is my Son, whom I love."

(Matthew 3:1–17; Mark 1:1–11; Luke 1:57–66; John 1:19–34)

THE TWELVE APOSTLES

Jesus traveled into Galilee to spread the Word of God. In every town he visited, crowds gathered to hear him preach. "The kingdom of God is near," he told them. "It is time to repent of your sins." One day, Jesus passed two fishermen casting their nets into the sea. They were Simon and his brother Andrew. "Leave your nets and follow me," Jesus told them. "I will make you fishers of men."

Simon and Andrew did as Jesus asked and became his first disciples. More disciples joined him as he traveled, and one day Jesus gathered them around him. From them he picked twelve to be his Apostles.

These twelve were Simon (known as Peter), his brother Andrew, James son of Zebedee, his brother John, Philip, Bartholomew, Matthew, Thomas, James, Thaddeus, Simon, and Judas Iscariot.

(Matthew 4:17–22; 10:1–4; Mark 1:14–20; 3:13–19; Luke 5:1–11; 6:12–16; 9:1)

THE WEDDING AT CANA

In the town of Cana, Jesus was invited to a wedding. The Apostles were with him, and so was Mary, his mother.

After some time, Mary saw that the wine had run out. She told Jesus, and Jesus told the servants to fill six large jars with water. "Now fill a cup and take it to the host." The servants did as he told them.

When the host drank from the cup, he turned to the bridegroom. "This wine is superb. Most people serve the best wine first and save the cheaper wine until the guests have drunk too much. But you have served your best wine last."

Then Mary, the servants, and the Apostles realized that Jesus had turned the water to wine. This was the first miracle that Jesus performed.

(John 2:1–11)

THE SERMON ON THE MOUNT

Word of Jesus spread throughout the land, and wherever he went, large crowds gathered to hear him. He healed the sick and brought comfort to the poor and needy.

He preached to them of the kingdom of God and how they could attain it. "Those who are sick or poor or hungry should rejoice, for they will receive their reward in heaven. But those who are rich and seek material gain on earth will find no comfort there."

He preached compassion, humility, and obedience to the commandments. Those who heard him were amazed by his words, for no one had ever spoken like him before.

*(**Matthew 5**:7; **Luke 6**:17–49)*

THE PARABLE OF THE PRODIGAL SON

Jesus often preached in parables, so that those who came to listen would more easily understand the Word of God. One day the lawyers were mocking him for welcoming the company of sinners. "One repentant sinner brings more rejoicing in heaven than ninety-nine good men who do not need forgiveness," Jesus told them.

"Once there was a man with two sons," he continued. "The younger asked for his share of money, then spent it recklessly. When he had none left, he decided to return to his father and beg forgiveness for his behavior. Humbly he went home and asked his father to treat him as a hired worker, for he was no longer to be called his son. But his father called for a great feast to celebrate his son's return. The elder son was angry because he had worked hard for his father but had never received such splendid treatment. 'My son,' explained the old man, 'we must celebrate because your brother was lost to us, and now he is found.'"

(Luke 15:1–32)

90

THE WORKERS IN THE VINEYARD

Jesus explained to his followers that those who trust in earthly possessions will not reap rewards in heaven. Then he told a parable that shows God gives according to grace, not merit.

"A landowner hired men to work in his vineyards and promised to pay them one coin," he told his listeners. "Toward the end of the day he saw men who still had no work and sent them to his vineyard too. When the work was finished, he paid his workers, beginning with those who had started last. He gave each of them one coin. Those who had worked since the beginning of the day expected more money. When he gave them one coin also, they grumbled that they had done more work than the others. The landowner explained that he would treat them all the same."

Jesus explained that no one gets less than he was promised. And all get more than they deserve.

(Matthew 19:23–30; 20:1–16)

THE GOOD SAMARITAN

One day while Jesus was preaching, a lawyer stood up and questioned him. "The Law says that we should love our neighbor as ourselves," said the lawyer. "But who is my neighbor?"

In reply Jesus said, "A man was traveling to Jerusalem when robbers attacked him and left him for dead. Several people saw the man, but although they followed the Law, they did nothing to help him. Instead they crossed to the other side of the road and passed him by.

"But then came a Samaritan, who was considered an outsider. He helped the man, treated his wounds, and took him to an inn to recover. The next day he had to leave, but he gave the innkeeper money to look after the injured man."

Jesus turned to the lawyer. "Which of these men was a true neighbor?" he asked. And the lawyer replied, "The man who helped." "Go then and do likewise," said Jesus.

*(**Luke 10**:25–37)*

THE PARABLE OF THE SOWER

When a large crowd had gathered, Jesus said to them, "A farmer went out to sow his seed. As he scattered it, some fell on the path and was eaten by birds. Some fell on rock, and the plants withered on the dry ground. Some seed fell among weeds that choked the plants. But some seed fell on good soil, and the plants grew strong and plentiful."

When the disciples asked Jesus what the parable meant, he explained to them: "The seed that falls on the path is like those who hear the Word of God but do not believe. The seed that falls on stony ground is like those who hear but do not maintain their faith. The seed choked by weeds represents people who get distracted by earthly worries.

"But the seed that falls on good soil stands for those who show their true conversion by maintaining their faith and producing the fruit of obedience."

(Matthew 13:4–9; Luke 8:1–15)

JESUS HEALS THE SICK

One day some men brought their crippled friend to see Jesus. This friend was paralyzed, and they carried him on a mat. There was such a crowd around Jesus that the men climbed up onto the roof and lowered their friend into the room below.

When Jesus saw how strong their faith was, he healed the crippled man. "Friend, your sins are forgiven," he said. "Take your mat and go home."

Another time a Roman soldier approached Jesus as he was entering a town. He told Jesus that his faithful servant was dying. "I will come to him," said Jesus. But the soldier replied, "I do not ask you to go to my home, for I am not worthy. But only say the word and my servant shall be healed."

"Never have I seen such faith as yours," said Jesus gladly. "Your servant shall live."

(Matthew 9:1–8; Luke 5:17–26; Matthew 8:5–13)

JESUS WALKS ON THE WATER

One day Jesus was teaching in a very remote place. As it grew dark, the Apostles told Jesus that he should send the people away. "They will be hungry soon, and we have nothing for them here."

But Jesus took five loaves and two small fish and divided them among the Apostles. "Pass this food around the crowd." The Apostles did not know what to think, for there were many people in the crowd. But they did as Jesus asked. To their amazement, there was plenty of food for everyone.

After this miracle, Jesus went to pray by himself. The Apostles took a boat to the other side of the lake, but a strong wind blew up, and they became worried.

Suddenly they saw Jesus walking toward them across the water. They were terrified, but Jesus called out to reassure them. "Come to me, Peter," he said. As soon as Peter stepped from the boat, he became afraid. "Help me, Lord!" he cried. "I will sink." Jesus helped Peter back on board. Jesus asked him, "Peter, why did you doubt?"

(Matthew 14:13–31; Mark 8:1–9; Luke 9:10-17; John 6:1–21)

THE TRANSFIGURATION

Jesus took three of his Apostles, Peter, James, and John, to the top of a high mountain. There Jesus was transfigured. His face shone as brilliantly as the sun, and his clothes became a blinding white. The prophets, Moses and Elijah, appeared beside him, bathed in the same light.

A bright cloud came down around them, and the Apostles heard the voice of God. "This is my beloved Son. Listen to him."

In terror the three Apostles fell to their knees. Jesus reached out to them and told them not to be afraid. "You must go back now. But do not speak of what you have seen here until the Son of man has risen again."

The Apostles left Jesus, puzzled by his last words.

(Matthew 17:1–9; Mark 9:2–13; Luke 9:28–36)

JESUS AND THE CHILDREN

Wherever Jesus went, parents brought their babies for him to touch and bless. Little children gathered around him as he preached, all trying to get as close to him as they could.

The apostles thought that the children were bothering Jesus by crowding him. They tried to chase the children away, but Jesus stopped them. "Let the little children come to me. You know that the kingdom of God welcomes the weak and the small. You have heard me say this many times."

He pointed to the smallest child playing at his feet. "You should all be more like this child," he said to the listening crowd. "It is only with a child's trust and simplicity that you shall enter the kingdom of God."

(Matthew 19:13–15; Mark 10:13–16; Luke 18:15–17)

LAZARUS

Lazarus, a friend of Jesus, was dying. His sisters, Mary and Martha, sent word to Jesus that he was ill. But when Jesus reached their home, Lazarus was already dead. Martha and Mary came to greet him. "Lord, if you had been with him when he was first ill," they sobbed, "he would have been healed." They took Jesus to the tomb where Lazarus had been laid to rest.

"Roll away the stone that covers the entrance," Jesus told them. Wondering, they did as he asked. Jesus looked up toward heaven: "Father, I know you have always heard my prayers. Now let everyone see that I do your will."

Jesus faced the tomb and cried, "Lazarus, come out!" In joy and amazement the people watched as Lazarus walked out of the tomb.

(John 11:1–43)

JESUS ENTERS JERUSALEM

Although many people now believed in Jesus and the kingdom of God, he had powerful enemies. The high priests and lawyers saw him as a threat to the ruling power of Rome. They tried to trap him with questions so that they could arrest him for stirring up rebellion. The people's love for him frightened them.

When the feast of Passover came, no one believed Jesus would go to Jerusalem. The Apostles begged him not to go. "You will surely be arrested," they cried. But they could not persuade him. Riding humbly on a donkey, Jesus entered the gates of Jerusalem.

Thousands had heard of his coming and lined the road as he passed. They spread palm leaves on the road before him and praised him as their Lord. "Blessed is he who comes in the name of God!" they cried.

(Matthew 21; Mark 11; 12:1–34; Luke 19:28–48; 20:1–39; John 7:25–44; 12:12–19)

THE LAST SUPPER

Jesus knew that in Jerusalem he would be betrayed and put to death. He warned the Apostles that this would be the last Passover feast he would share with them.

That evening, Jesus and his Apostles met in the room prepared for their meal. They were horrified when he told them, "This is the last night I will eat this bread and drink this wine. Tonight I will be arrested."

Then he took some bread, broke it into pieces, and divided it among the Apostles. "This is my body," he told them. "I offer it as a sacrifice for all mankind. Eat it in memory of me."

Then he filled a glass with wine. "This is my blood," he said, passing it to each Apostle in turn. "It will be shed for you and for all men. Drink this in memory of me."

(Matthew 16:21–28; 20:17–19; 26:17–30; Mark 8:31–38; 10:32–34; 14:12–26; Luke 18:31–34; 22:7–23; John 12:20–36; 13:18–21)

THE BETRAYAL

Jesus knew one of his closest friends would betray him. Judas Iscariot had been tempted by Satan and agreed to betray Jesus in return for thirty pieces of silver.

After the Last Supper, Jesus went to pray in the Garden of Gethsemene. A band of soldiers arrived, led by Judas. "You should arrest the man I greet with a kiss," he told them. He went to Jesus and kissed him. "Have you betrayed me, Judas?" Jesus asked him sorrowfully. The other Apostles wanted to fight so that Jesus could escape, but he went with the soldiers calmly.

Alone in the garden, Judas suddenly realized the terrible thing he had done. Crying out in horror, he threw the thirty pieces of silver to the ground in disgust. He could not live with the guilt of his betrayal and hanged himself.

*(**Matthew 26**:14–16; **26**:36–56; **27**:1–10; **Mark 14**:32–50; **Luke 22**:1–6; **22**:39–54; **John 18**:1–12)*

113

JESUS BEFORE PILATE

Jesus was taken before the high council, known as the Sanhedrin. They questioned him harshly about his teachings and asked him if he were the Son of God. "Yes, it is as you say," replied Jesus.

The council accused Jesus of blasphemy and took him to the Roman governor, Pontius Pilate. Pilate also asked Jesus if he were the King of the Jews. Again Jesus replied, "Yes, it is as you say." The Sanhedrin demanded that Jesus be put to death, but Pilate could see no reason for such harshness.

At that time it was the custom for one prisoner to be released during the Passover festival. Jesus and a vicious criminal called Barabbas were the only prisoners. When Pilate asked whom he should release, the crowd called for Barabbas.

Pilate tried to reason with the council and the crowd, but they demanded Jesus' death so strongly that at last he gave in to them. Jesus was led away to be crucified.

(Matthew 26:57–68; 27:11–26; Mark 14:53–65; 15:1–15; Luke 22:66–71; 23:1–25; John 18:28–40; 19:1–16)

CARRYING THE CROSS

As the soldiers led Jesus out of the governor's palace, they mocked him cruelly. They beat him and spat at him and placed a crown of thorns upon his head.

"Hail, King of the Jews!" they laughed.

The cross was brought forward, and Jesus was made to carry it on his shoulders through the streets. The soldiers forced a man called Simon, from Cyrene, to help Jesus bear the weight.

A large crowd followed Jesus, many of them weeping for him. "Do not weep for me," Jesus told them. "You should be weeping for yourselves and for your children, for there is much suffering ahead for you."

(Matthew 27:13–32; Mark 15:21–22; Luke 23:26–31; John 19:16–17)

THE CRUCIFIXION

The place of execution was called Golgotha, or Place of the Skull. Here the soldiers nailed Jesus to the cross and crucified him. Two robbers were crucified with him at the same time.

Above Jesus' head hung a sign that said, "The King of the Jews." The priests and lawyers came to mock Jesus. "He is the Son of God," they laughed. "And he cannot even save himself!"

After Jesus had hung on the cross for many hours, a heavy darkness spread across the land. Suddenly Jesus cried out, "My God, why have you forsaken me?" The crowd waited in awe to see what would happen.

Jesus cried out once more to God, then his spirit left him, and he died. At the same moment the earth shook, and the temple curtain tore in two. The followers of Jesus took him down from the cross and laid him in a tomb.

(Matthew 27:32–56; Mark 15:21–41; Luke 23:26–49; John 19:18–42)

THE RESURRECTION

After three days had passed, Mary Magdalene, one of the disciples, visited Jesus' tomb. To her dismay the tomb was open and the body of Jesus was missing. As she began to weep at her loss, a shining angel appeared. "You should not be unhappy," it said. "You should be glad because Jesus has risen from the dead."

Then a voice called to her, and a man stood before her. At first she did not recognize him. Then to her great amazement and joy, her eyes were opened, and she saw that it was Jesus.

Full of awe and wonder, she hurried into town to tell the other disciples. Although Jesus had told them that the Son of God must die and rise again, they had not truly believed it.

*(**Matthew 28**:1–10; **Mark 16**:1–11; **Luke 24**:1–12; **John 20**:1–18)*

THE REVELATION

Later that same day, Jesus appeared to two of his disciples as they traveled to Emmaus. They did not recognize him, but welcomed him as a traveling companion. "We were just speaking about Jesus of Nazareth," they told him. "We hoped that he would be the savior of the Jews, but the council arrested and crucified him. Some have claimed to have seen him risen from the tomb, but this cannot be true."

Jesus rebuked them for their lack of faith. "Was it not foretold that the Son of God must die, then rise again?" he asked them. In wonder they recognized him, but he disappeared before them.

That evening Jesus appeared to the Apostles. Even they did not believe he had risen from the dead and were afraid, thinking he was a ghost. "Touch me," he told them. "See the wounds in my hands and feet. I am no ghost."

(Mark 16:12–14; Luke 24:13–48; John 19:30)

THE ASCENSION

The Apostles went out to the Mount of Olives, where they had once prayed with Jesus. There he appeared to them for the last time. "You must prepare," he told them. "The Holy Spirit will soon come upon you. On that day you must go out and spread the Word of God to all nations. You must teach mankind all that you have seen and learned while I was with you."

Jesus then blessed the Apostles, who bowed their heads in worship. He rose into the sky, went into a cloud, and ascended into heaven, to sit at God's right hand.

And just as Jesus had said, the Holy Spirit came upon the Apostles and gave them the strength and wisdom to go out and preach the Word of God.

Wherever they traveled many listened, many believed, and many were saved, just as Jesus had foretold.

(Matthew 28:16–20; Mark 16:15–20; Luke 24:44–53; John 20:21)